Large Print Coloring Book for Adults of

Summer

ZenMaster Coloring Books

Copyright © 2018 by ZenMaster
All rights reserved. No part of this publication may be reproduced, distributed, or transmitted in any form or by any means, including photocopying, recording, or other electronic or mechanical methods, without the prior written permission of the publisher.

Helpful Tips for Coloring

~ Sometimes the colors appear differently on paper than what you would expect. Use the color test page to play with your colors beforehand.

~ If you are using colored pencils make sure to keep them sharp. This helps when coloring smaller areas or details on the page. Fine point sharpies also work great for smaller areas.

~ Speaking of sharpies, make sure you put a scrap piece of paper behind the page you are coloring to keep the markers from bleeding to the next page.

~ When using crayons or pencils start out light. You can always go back and darken later.

~ There are so many tools for coloring: markers, sharpies, crayons, pencils, pastels, and the list goes on. Experiment with what works best for you and your designs. Though it's not necessary, using higher quality coloring utensils makes a difference.

~ If you come to a design that seems overwhelming just pick a place to start and go from there. Once you begin your creativity will quickly take over!! If you get discouraged just take a break and come back to the page later.

~ Remember to practice. Like anything else, the more you do it the better you'll get. It'll become more and more relaxing each time.

~ DON'T FOLLOW THE RULES! It's up to you how you color your designs. Just let your creativity take the lead and HAVE FUN!

COLOR TEST PAGE

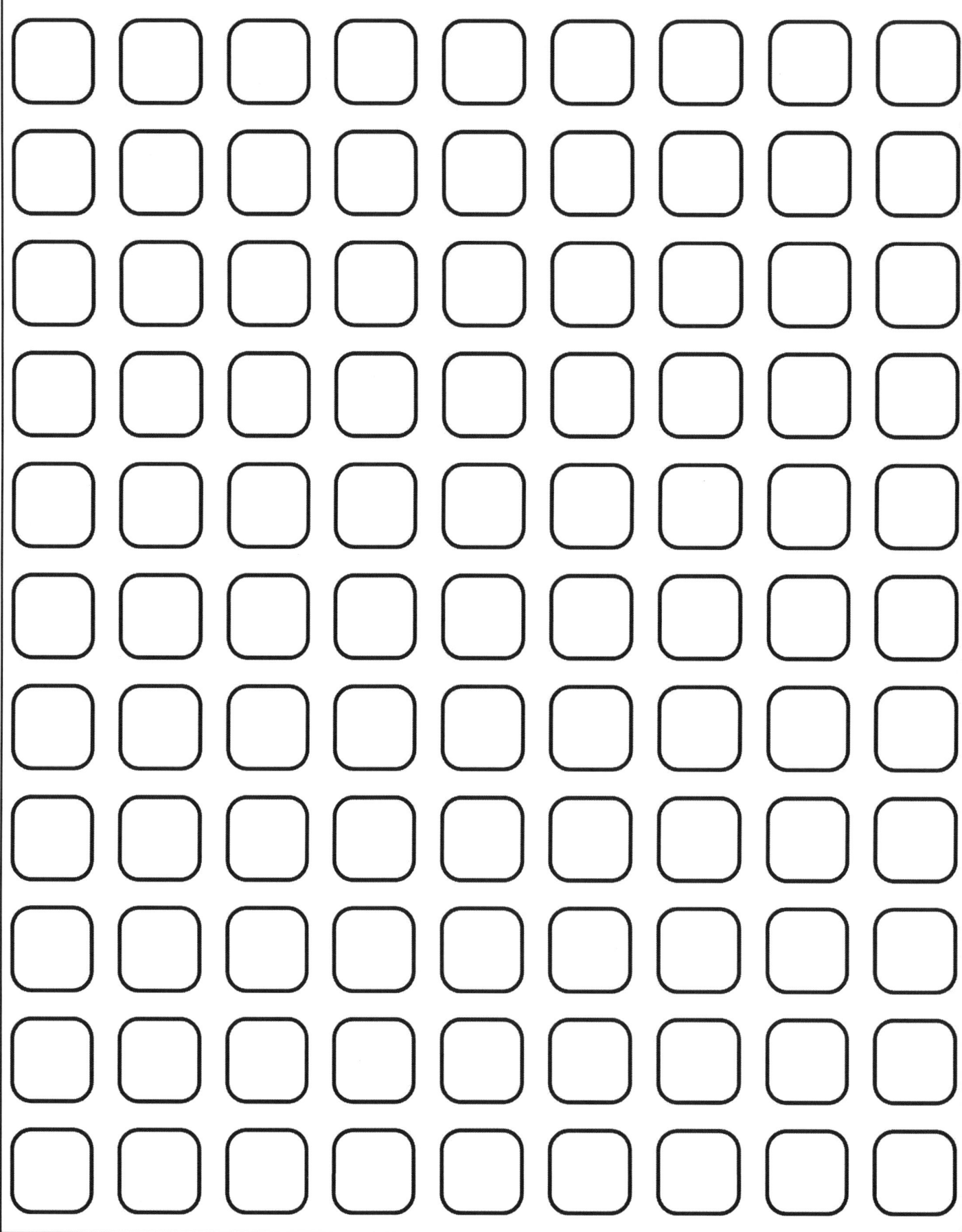

COLOR TEST PAGE

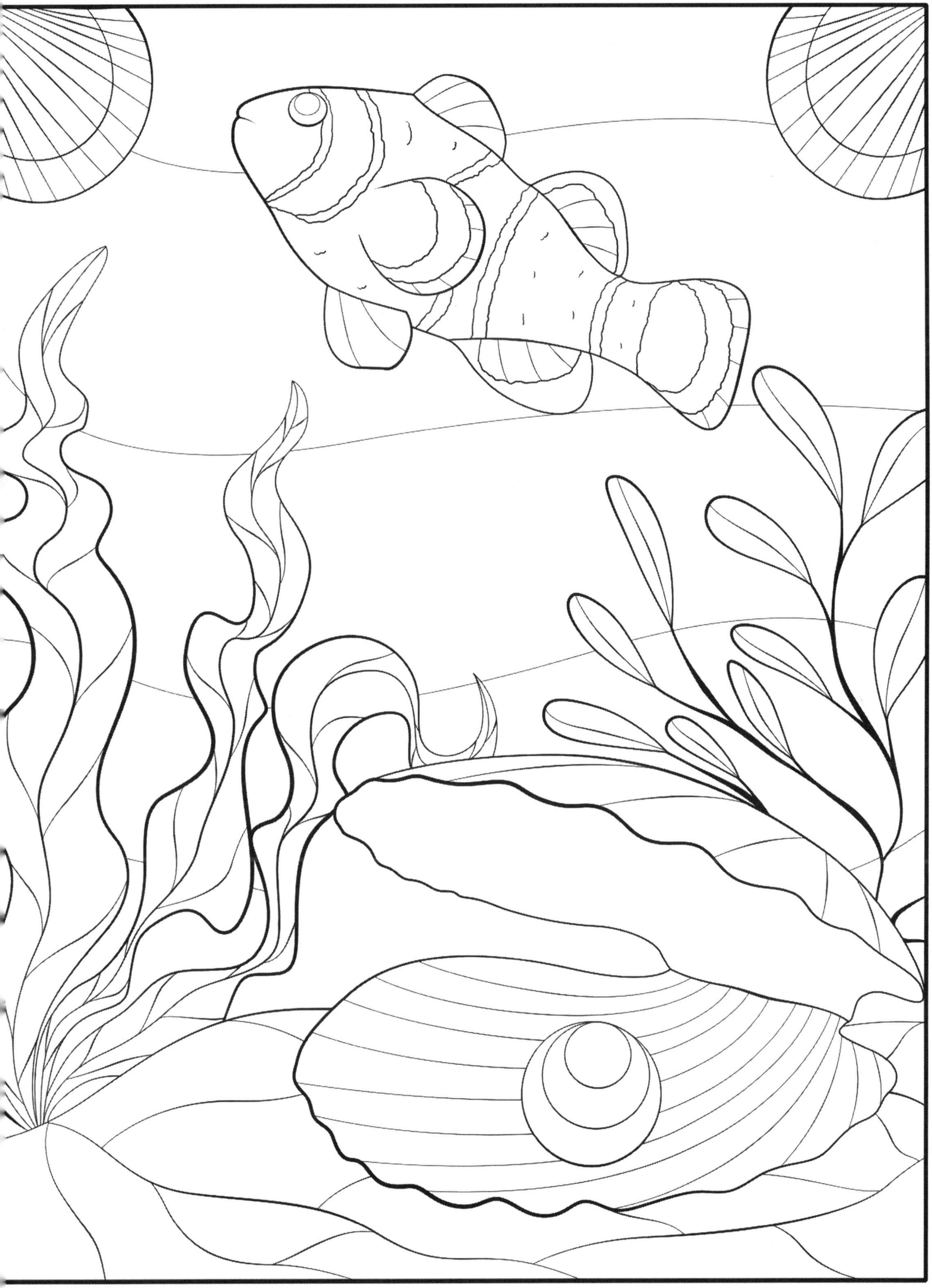

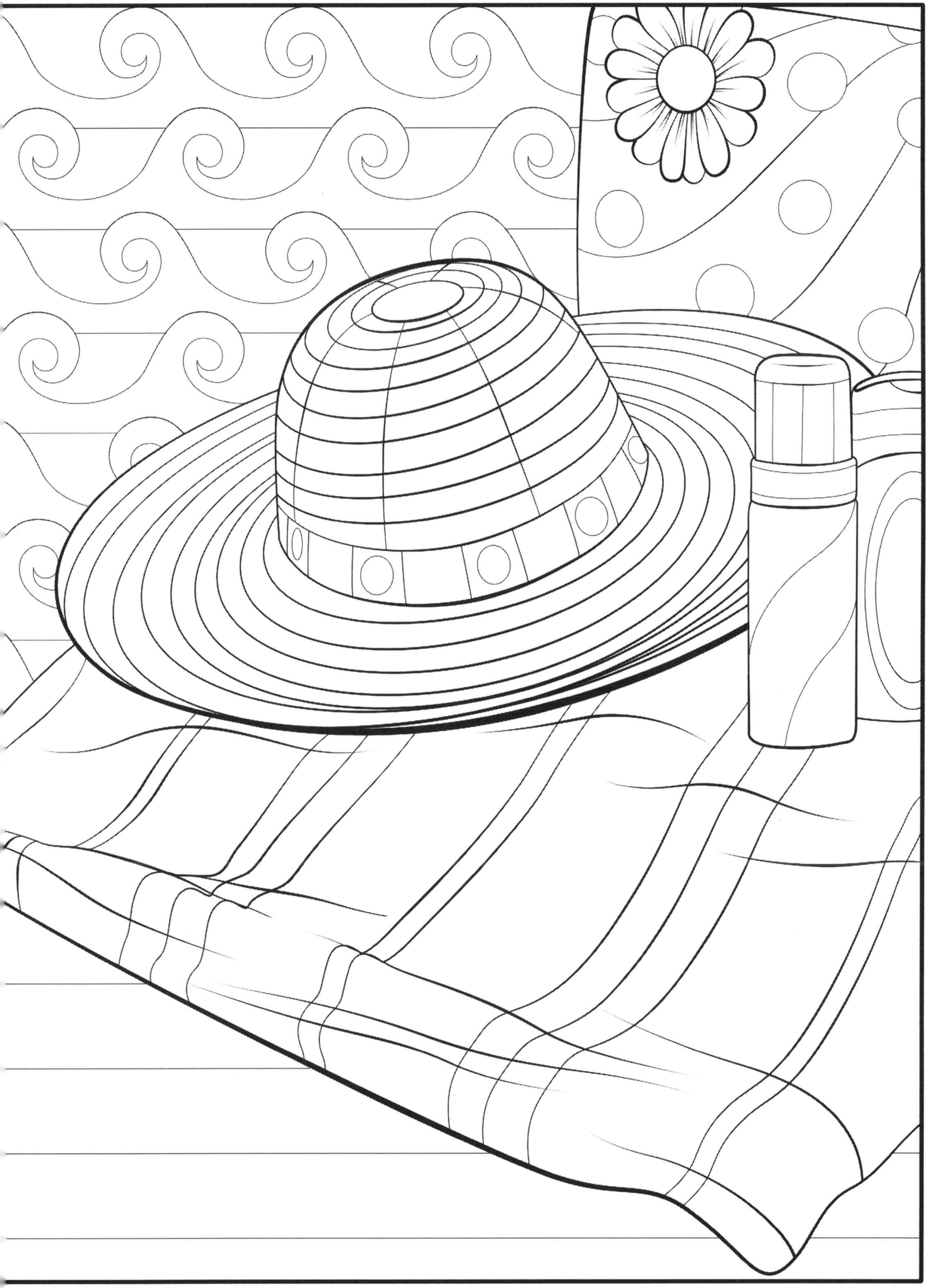

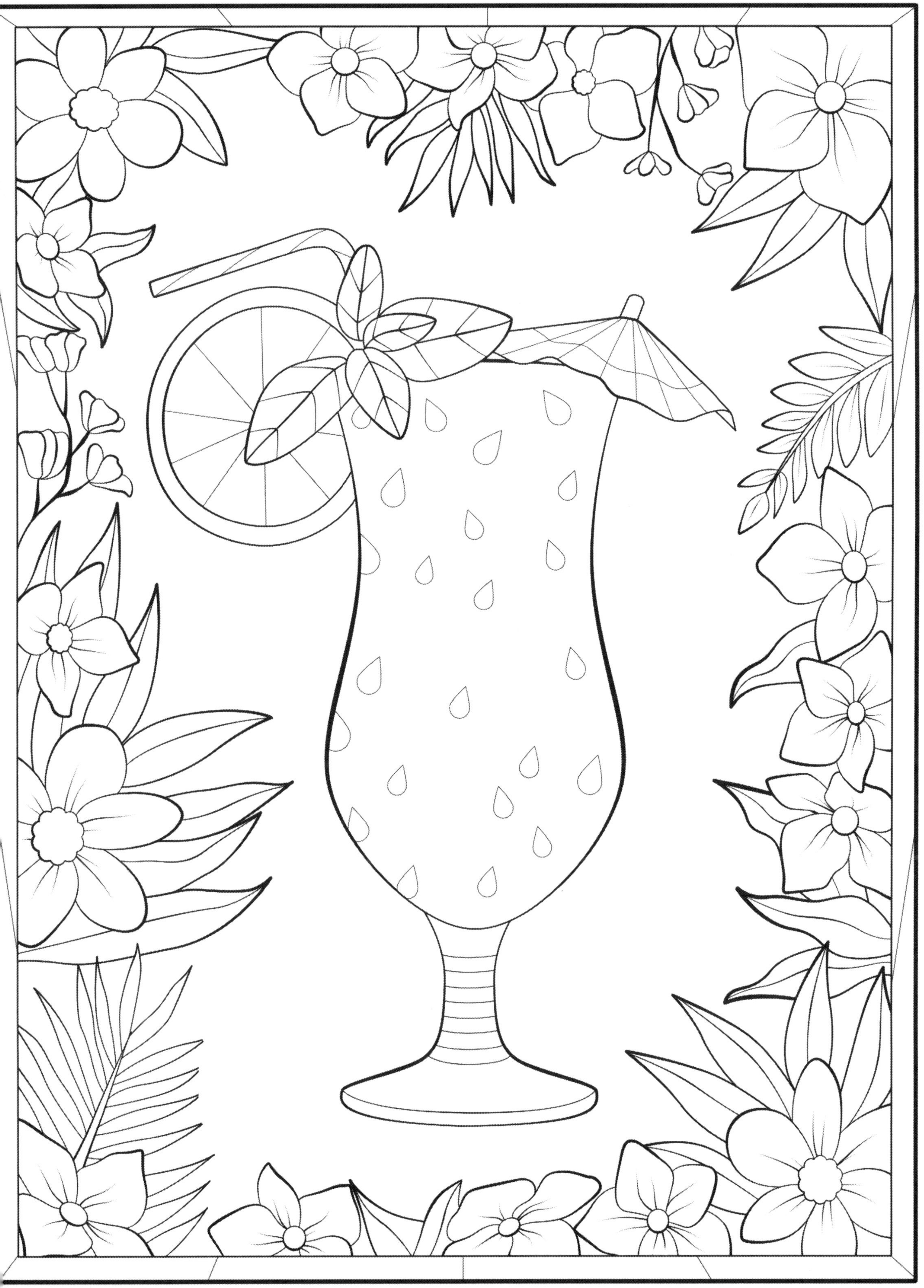

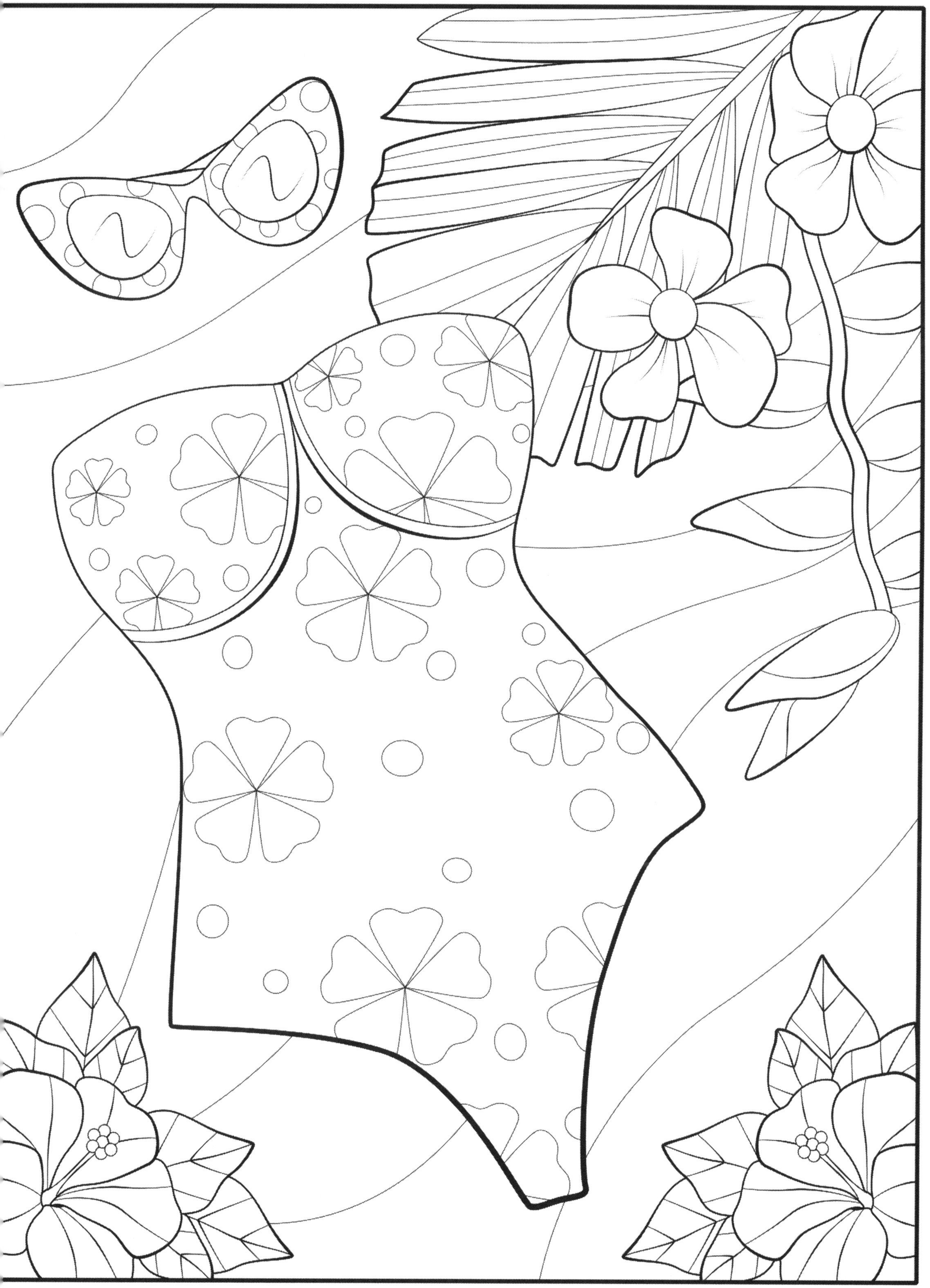

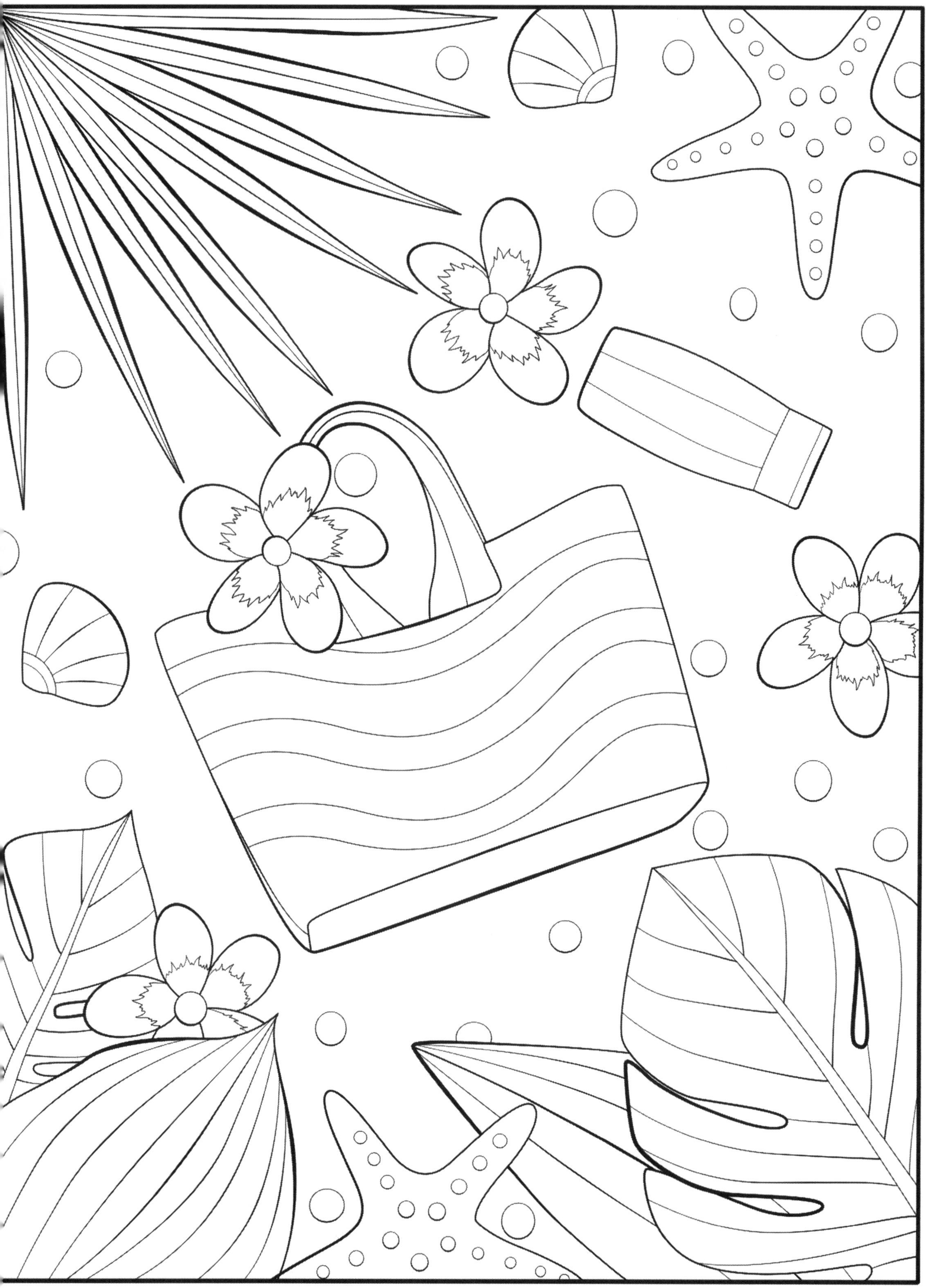

Thank you for supporting
ZenMaster Coloring Books!

I aim to make sure my customers have the most enjoyable and relaxing coloring experience possible and I would love to hear your feedback!

Please leave a review on Amazon and follow me on facebook for updates and free coloring pages!

https://www.facebook.com/zenmastercoloringbooks/

check out more of my books at:

amazon.com/author/zenmastercoloringbooks

Free Bonus Page!
from:

Winter Wonderland

latge print coloring book for adults

https://amzn.com/7724506

Also available in color by numbers!!
https://amzn.com/1979269661

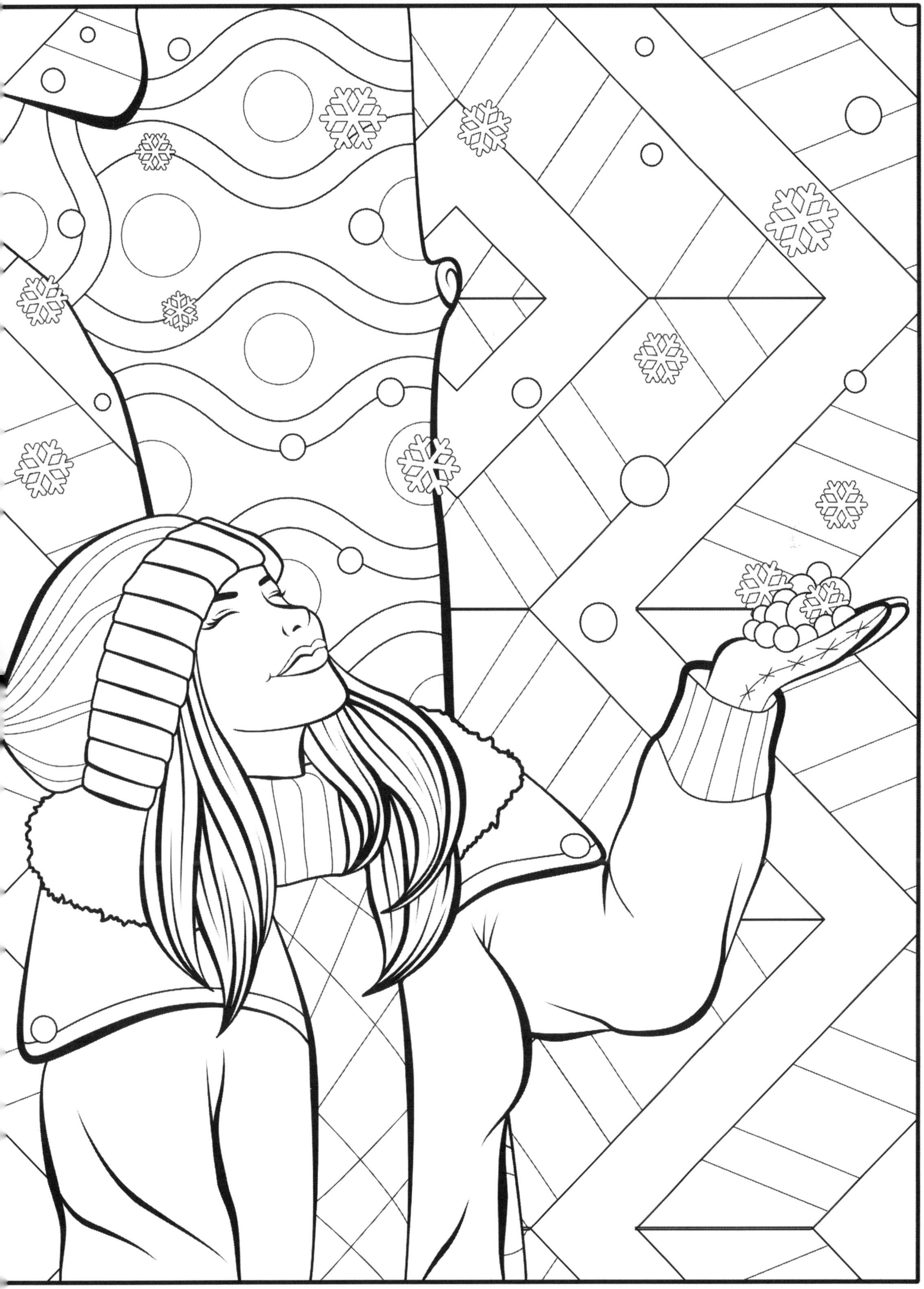

Free Bonus Page!
from:

Large Print Adult Coloring Book of
Spring

https://amzn.com/1985347024

Also available in color by numbers!!
https://amzn.com/1985375540

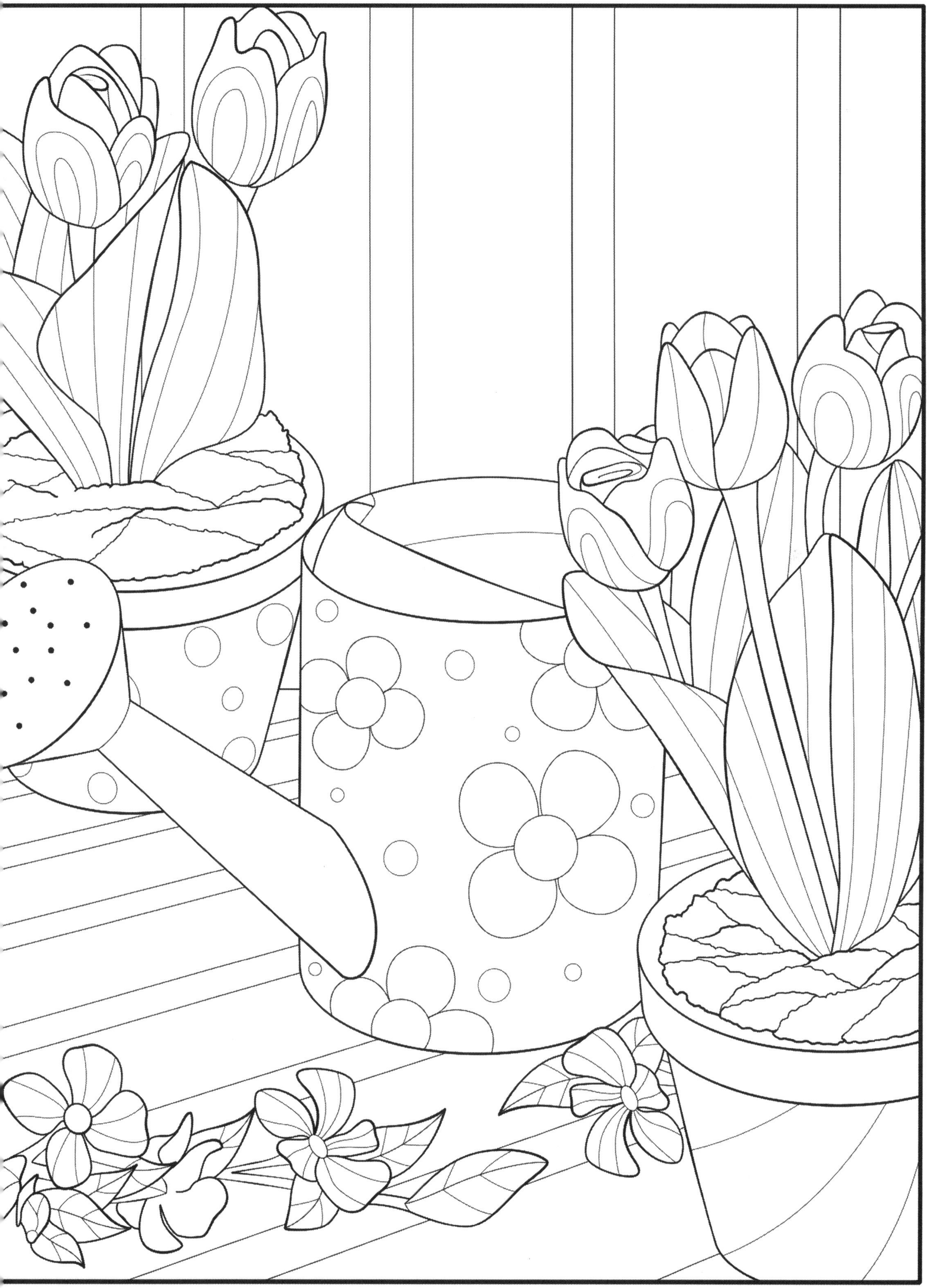

Free Bonus Page!
from:

Easy Adult Color By Numbers Coloring Book of
Fall

https://amzn.com/171861506X

Also available in color by numbers!!
https://amzn.com/1718823037

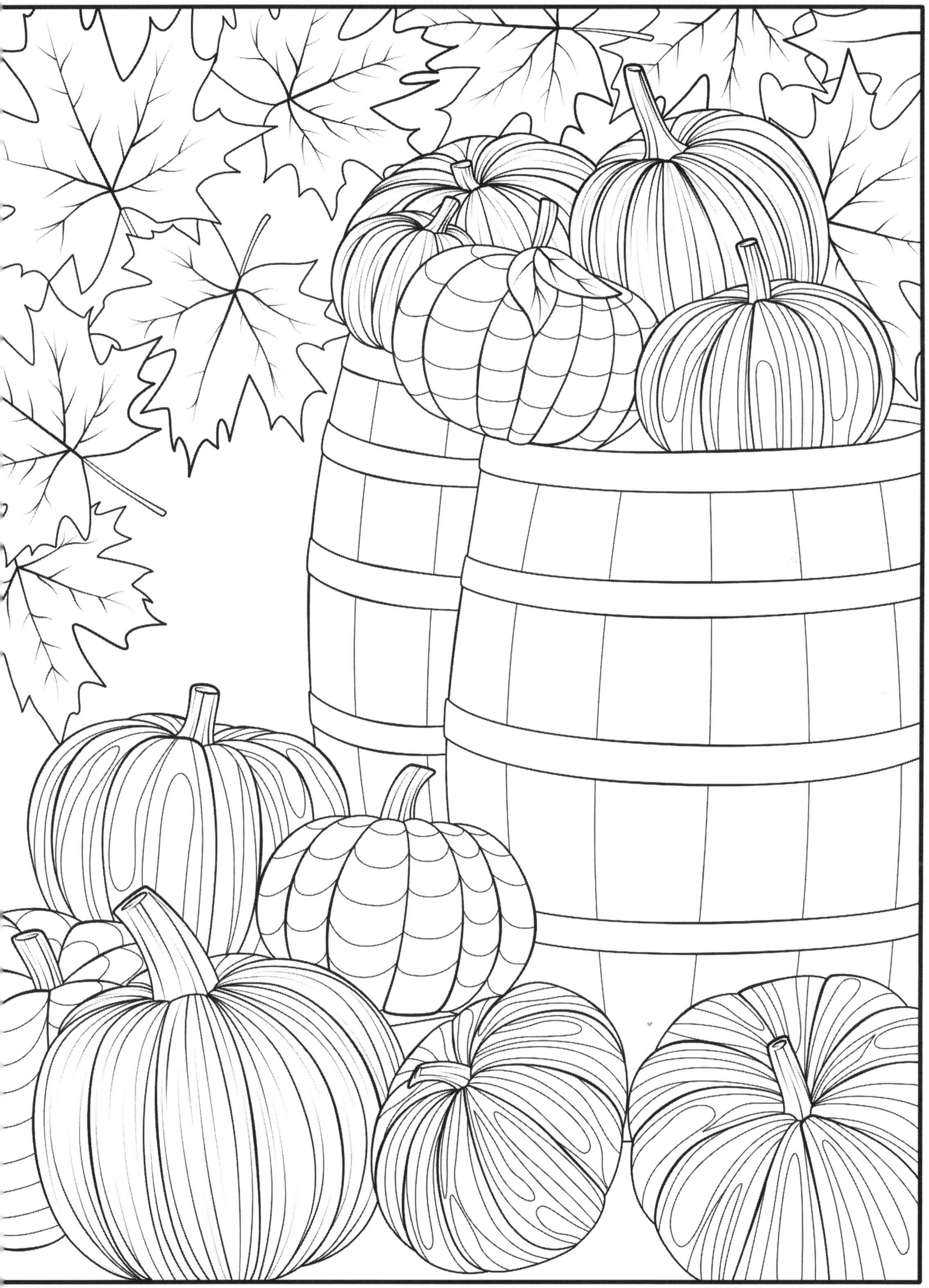

BONUS PAGE! From "Zen Coloring Notebook"

Made in the USA
Middletown, DE
11 May 2020